REFRESH, REFILL, RENEW

A 30-DAY DEVOTIONAL

DARLENE THORNE

A HEART AFTER THE FATHER, LLC

Refresh, Refill, Renew

Copyright © 2019 by Darlene Thorne

Published by A Heart After the Father, LLC

Publishing information address:

A Heart After the Father, LLC

817 Parkridge Drive

Clayton, North Carolina 27527

www.darlenethorne.com

All rights reserved, including the right of reproduction in whole or in part of any form.

No part of this publication may be stored in any retrieval system or transmitted in any form or by electronic, mechanical, photocopying, recording or otherwise without written permission except in the case of brief quotations embodied in critical articles or reviews.

For information about special discounts for bulk purchases, please contact the author at ladydarlenelt@gmail.com.

Manufactured and printed in the United States of America

Unless otherwise identified, Bible quotations in this volume are from the New International Version of the Bible.

ISBN:978-0-9960498-4-9

I would like to dedicate this book to my family for all of your support. I love you all to life!

PART I
REFRESH

DAY ONE

Psalm 19:7 - "The law of the Lord is perfect refreshing the soul; the statutes of the Lord are trustworthy making wise the simple."

Abba's law makes us more like Him if we apply it to our hearts. Our responsibility is to carry out His word because when we do, our lives get better for doing it. It brings us to another level of maturity we lack because Abba will bring to us what we need. As we reside in His presence daily, our steps will be ordered by Him. Surely, our souls will be satisfied. We can trust His word. We can trust in Him to do what He says He will do. He may tell to do something that inner minds may be unconventional about, but when we know it is coming from Him, it will all work out for our good. Sometimes it may feel like we are walking a path no one else is going down, but if we keep trusting in the leading of Holy Spirit and even if pope think we are going in a different direction, we can trust and believe the leading of the Lord will result in Him being glorified.

We will receive unusual wisdom from on high! Thank you Father for knowing better than me!

DAY TWO

Psalm 68:9 - "You gave abundant showers of God; you refreshed your weary inheritance."

WE ARE HIS WEARY INHERITANCE. YES, ABBA SHOWERED UPON US A NEW joy, peace, love, mercy and grace. At times when we become tired, frustrated and at a loss, there comes our Daddy God intervening on our behalf. He overshadows us and gives us exactly what we need to continue the journey. Just as He refreshed Elijah when he was at his lowest point, our Father will always refresh us. He does not just sprinkle refreshment, he does because it is in abundance! Overflowing with the things we need, we do not need to worry or fear - Abba is always there. What are you lacking? What do you need? Abba has it!

One thing is necessary from you though- Just ask Him for the refreshing. Seek His face and worship Him. Open your heart and tell Him what you need. He is ready to open the windows and pour out in abundance the refreshment for your soul.

DAY THREE

Proverbs 11:25 - "A generous person will prosper. Whoever refreshes others will be refreshed."

DON'T BE SELFISH. DO YOU REALIZE THAT IF YOU GIVE, YOU OPEN YOURSELF up to receive? It is like planting a seed, you always reap more than you sow. The apple tree that started out as a seed gives shade to many and its fruit provides sustenance for those who partake of it. Then the tree is replenished with more fruit to refresh others.

The more you are generous and help to bring hope, health and healing to someone else, you reap that and more for your soul. It's not strange that when you bless someone with something you feel really good after you have done it.

I remember the first time my husband and I gave our first earnings, what we called a "big seed" to someone. We prayed about it and became obedient to give. We wrote the check and gave it to them. The way I felt after that was absolutely amazing! As we refresh someone else, our souls are blessed! Reflect on how you can be a blessing to someone today.

DAY FOUR

Acts 3:19 - "Repent, then, and turn to God, so that your sins may be wiped out, that times of refreshing may come from the Lord."

WE MISS THE MARK SOMETIMES AND INSTEAD OF IMMEDIATELY REPENTING, we try to hide from the reality. Why we do that is a mystery to me because He sees all and knows when we are disobedient. Nothing can be hidden from Him. We tend to do things like, stay away from attending church, avoid reading our Bibles, not watching uplifting messages and one of the biggest things we do is avoid talking to our believer friends because we don't want to have to explain ourselves to them. But this scripture is clear - if we would simply repent and turn to Abba, He will blot out our sins and make us whole. He will cleanse our hearts and the time of refreshing will be so sweet. He loves us deeply and He's always with us. Run to Him and receive the refreshment of forgiveness.

DAY FIVE

Jeremiah 31:25 - "I will refresh the weary and satisfy the faint."

THIS IS GOD'S PROMISE TO US. HE WILL REFRESH US. HE WILL SATISFY US. When our inner spirit becomes tired, especially those times when our strength becomes limited, His love is sufficient. We, at times, become so busy doing life that we just forget to rest. We are too preoccupied with the activities of the day that we do not give quality time on the things that are most important to us. We must give ourselves to keeping our eyes fixed on the things that will bring eternal value and not temporary satisfaction. We then give Abba the ability to minister to our spirit and refresh us when we do become weary, however, we are weary for the right reasons. Our true satisfaction will come from above which only Abba gives. We will not lack in any good thing because our Father will satisfy our souls.

DAY SIX

Romans 15:32 - "…so that I may come to you with joy, by God's will, and in your company be refreshed,"

I HAVE THE JOY, JOY, JOY, JOY DOWN IN MY HEART TO STAY (GEORGE William Cooke).

God gives us joy! Abba fills us when we come into His presence, our souls are built up because we have been with Him. Nehemiah 8:10 part B states that 'the joy of the Lord is your strength.' We are to be joyous - filled! Nehemiah is telling the people to enjoy food and share with others. He told them not to be sad and full of grief because the joy of the Lord becomes is their strength. When you are refreshed, you are strengthened. You now have the ability to complete the next assignment. You are better prepared for what is to come. You think clearer and can be better equipped for fulfilling your God given task.

DAY SEVEN

II Timothy 1:16 - "May the Lord show mercy to the household of Onesiphorus - because he often refreshed me and was not ashamed of my chains."

Onesiphorus, his name means "Profit." He stayed with Paul, and supported him through all of his journey. He went out of his way to find and visit Paul when he was in prison. Why did this guy feel the need to be there for Paul? Well, as history reveals, Paul brought the good news of the gospel to the church in Ephesus and that is where Onesiphorus is from. Perhaps, he was so grateful that his way of expressing his thanks was to always be there for Paul.

Are we an Onesiphorus for someone we are thankful for taking time to minister to us? How can we show them that we appreciate them? What can we do to bring refreshment to someone's soul? Just as this young man met Paul and went out of his way to bring refreshment to him when he was in prison, we should minister to someone who helped us when they may be in need. We cannot hold back from being a blessing to someone who has been a blessing to us.

DAY EIGHT

Psalm 23: 2, 3 - "He makes me to lie down in green pastures, He leads me beside the still waters. He restores my soul. He leads me in the path of righteousness for His names' sake."

GOD GIVES US STRENGTH. WHEN WE COME INTO HIS PRESENCE, IT IS LIKE lying in the green pastures. Usually, when you drive down a road where it is just green grass for days it looks so luscious and peaceful. It is unbothered and appears inviting, like you could just walk through it for days. The sun shines on the grass and it looks like a green river. The presence of the Lord is so comforting, sweet, and gracious.

The still waters - the complete presence of God overtaking me. I feel enveloped in His love. This is so serene. Sometimes, I weep in adoration for the one who gave all He had - His only begotten Son just for me and He daily loads me with the benefits attached with redemption! Take time to reflect on His benefits. I just want to begin with life itself! Breathing with my lungs, seeing, hearing, tasting, the ability to move are just a few benefits. Yes, benefits that we take for granted that we are to automatically have these things. Life and health are the real benefits we enjoy from God! I am thankful for the movement. The ability to do for myself! Wow! Thank you, Lord! Oh yes, back to breathing - I was born with a condition called asthma. At 9 months old I was hospitalized because I had a very bad attack. But, I lived! Growing up, there were many days lost from school due to those attacks. Now for some, they took it for granted running and playing because they could do it without getting sick. So for me to breathe? It was and daily is a benefit! What are you thankful for? What are the benefits for which you are grateful? Our Father desires to speak to us - let's remain quiet enough as we are in the 'pastures' of His presence to reflect on His benefits toward us.

DAY NINE

Proverbs 3:7, 8 - "Be not wise in your own eyes fear the Lord and turn away from evil. It will be healing for your flesh and refreshment to your bones."

EVER BEEN IN THE PRESENCE OF A KNOW-IT-ALL? YOU KNOW THE ONE WHO has been everywhere and done everything? Oh yes, those folk can be a turn off. But how many times do we attempt to live our lives like we know more than the one who created us? We think we have it all figured out and we fall flat on our faces we those conditions hit us hard. Abba stands waiting for us to turn to Him so that He will first heal our wounds, heal our hearts and then refresh us so we can go back and complete the task the way He designed us to complete it.

Sometimes, our feelings get hurt when we mess up and others see it. We want to run and hide and we vow to never do anything again. It is so because we attempted to do it without first getting our direction from the Lord on how to do it.

For those who are yet to come to the Lord may say something like,

"When I get myself together, I will get saved or I will get it right with the man upstairs." How many times have we heard that? We do not have to do anything but just come to Him. It is almost like washing the dishes and then putting them in the dishwasher.

Let's reflect on that song, 'What can wash away my sins? Nothing but the blood of Jesus; what can make me whole again? Nothing but the blood of Jesus!' It is His blood and His power that makes the difference in our lives.

DAY TEN

> I Corinthians 16:18 - "For they refresh my spirit as well as yours. Give recognition to such men."

PAUL IS TALKING ABOUT THE MEN FROM THE CHURCH OF CORINTH, AND according to Jill Gill's Exposition of the Bible, he said that, 'by their coming and their presence; the very sight of them gave him joy and pleasure.' Have you been a breath of fresh air to someone? When you come into their presence do they breathe a sigh of relief and have a smile on their face that they get to spend time with you? Are you the one that brings joy to the heart of another?

Let me encourage you today to look to be that for someone this week. Ask the Lord to show you who it is so you can refresh them. Maybe it is picking up a $5 gift card from the local coffee shop or inviting them out for dinner to your home or going out. Something that helps to revive the soul of another. It may even be helping them clean their house or garage, you get the idea. Spend time with someone else and bring refreshment to their spirit. When all is said and done, you too will be refreshed!

PART II
REFILL

DAY ONE

Psalm 81:10 - "For it was I the Lord your God who rescued you from the land of Egypt. Open your mouth wide and I will fill it with good things."

When we want to stay healthy as our top priority, all we should do is to take a good look at our food choices. We are usually encouraged to keep a journal of what we eat. Then, we are really able to see what is good and the not so good things we are consuming. Good food choices will equate to a healthier body.

However, in order for us to really achieve the best results for a healthy body, we need to look at what we eat and then we must choose to make changes; behave to speak to our bodies. We speak to our bodies and tell our body that we are not giving into the cravings or the fast food on the way home. I remember talking to myself saying, "I have better food to eat at home." I would actually say it out loud! That did produce good results. If we want good results, we have to fill our mouths with good things.

As in the natural, so it goes in the spiritual. We must fill our mouth with the word. Speaking the word on a daily basis, multiple times on a daily basis, multiple times in a day, we 'feed' our spirit. Our soul is satisfied with the things of God. This brings about change and good things result from it. We are closer to the Lord, we hear His voice clearer and our direction is set because we can sense His presence. We understand this leading and we are changed. Daily filling is necessary, just like when we eat in the natural, we will be fed with the word of God and continue to be filled with His word for spiritual nourishment. What are you going to eat today?

DAY TWO

Psalm 103:5 - "He fills my life with good things so that my youth is renewed like eagles."

ALLOW ME TO SHARE WITH YOU SOME FACTS ABOUT THE EAGLE. THE EAGLE lives a pretty long life; 38 years is about the life span of the winged creation. When they mate, they mate for life! They find their companion when they are about 4 or 5 years old and they pair up till the end. These birds are also very nurturing for their offspring. They take care in teaching them to fly and it is amazing how they care for one another. They work together in building their home or nest. They build a pretty large nests, some 2 to 5 feet wide and a bit more than a foot deep. A really interesting fact about the eagle is that they have a see-through eyelid called a nictitating membrane that allows them to protect their eye and still maintains their vision. Eagles have sharp vision, and they can see further than most with such clarity.

With the characteristics of an eagle, isn't it beautiful that the writer speaks of us being renewed with the qualities of such a bird? God desires that we have long life and live in community with others. We also help to grow someone else by using our gifts to challenge and empower other to do the same.

There is nothing coincidental about the writer using the eagle as the comparison. When we understand their characteristics, we will want to emulate some of them in our lives. How are we like the eagle? Which of their characteristics do you want to emulate? It is truly possible. Ask the Holy Spirit to work it in you. He wants us to grow in Him and we have the right to ask what we will of Him. God is faithful to work through us and to mature us. Oh, to be renewed like the eagle - fearless, tenacious, a visionary and gentle with those called to us.

DAY THREE

Psalm 107:9 - "For He satisfies the thirsty and fills the hungry with good things."

WHEN WE ARE HUNGRY, HE FEEDS US. WHEN WE ARE THIRSTY, HE quenches that thirst! And to think that He would do this for us at all times! He told us to seek Him and we will find Him when we do it with our whole heart. There is no good thing He will withhold from those who walk up rightly. Oh, we have the privilege to ask and know that we shall receive. Wow! He longs to provide us with the meat and drink that will satisfy our souls. He satisfies us with good things. Good means to be desired or approved of; it also means that which is morally right, and righteous. We are given those things that are desirable and righteous. We will never lack in any good thing for that which Abba will provide. Relax in Him knowing that all our needs will be met and there is nothing our Father cannot do. He fills meaning to put into as much as can be held or conveniently contained; to cause to swell. Let our hearts swell up with satisfaction that comes from Abba.

DAY FOUR

Luke 1:41 - "At the sound of Mary's greeting Elizabeth's child leaped within her; and Elizabeth was filled with the Holy Spirit."

HAVE YOU EVER HEAR SOME NEWS THAT MADE YOU SO EXCITED THAT YOU screamed or jumped up and down? Did such news ever caused you to want to cry tears of joy because you were so elated? Well, that is what happened with Mary and Elizabeth. Whatever Mary said when she entered Elizabeth's presence brought so much joy that the baby she was carrying leaped! I personally believe that babies in the womb home can hear and I've got to believe the sound of Mary's voice coming into Elizabeth's home sparked something in little John!

What about you? What are you carrying? What people are you surrounding yourself with to continue ministering life to what you are about to birth? It is vital that those you choose to have around you are bringing you strength and not stress. Check your environment - is it toxic or is it life-giving? You want to be intentional that you will close the door to those things and people that are life zappers. They mean you no good and make your birthing process more difficult. It is okay to separate yourself from that for this season. You will be better and your delivery will be stress free. It is enough to giving birth to a dream/vision because it carries its own challenges, and you can choose to separate from the stressors to be free to deliver!

DAY FIVE

Exodus 34:6 - "The Lord passed infant of Moses; calling out, 'Yahweh! The Lord! The God of compassion and mercy! I am slow to anger and filled with unfailing love and faithfulness."

HE NEVER RUNS OUT OF WHAT WE NEED! ABBA'S SUPPLY IS DEEP AND endless! "Your love never fails never gives up, never runs out on me!" We sing that song in worship times but do we truly believe it? We must truly come in agreement with His word. His love does not fail - we must choose to accept this and know that even if we make a mistake that all is not lost and we have a Father who is always looking out for us. Our Father is full of compassion and mercy. He walks with us through the hard seasons of our lives. Sometimes, He is truly carrying us through. When we are at our weakest, He comes to our rescue.

When we disobey Abba like Jonah did, who went his way instead of obeying God - He still had mercy and did not take Jonah out! He gave him the opportunity to repent and do what he was assigned to do. Jonah repented and did do what God had initially instructed him to do. God is faithful to give us just what we need. His forgiveness covers us and He sets us on the right path so we can carry out our assignment.

Thank you Abba for your faithfulness!

DAY SIX

Psalm 119:64 - "Oh Lord, your unfailing love fills the earth; teach me your decrees:"

THINK ABOUT OUR WORLD; IT IS FILLED WITH PERPETUALNESS - THE SEASONS come, winter, spring, summer and fall in a continuum. Our Father makes sure that we have enough water for the plants to grow. Has there ever been a year where you go into a grocery store and do not see any vegetables? No, there may be seasonal vegetation but never will you walk in a store a store and you won't be able to get what you need. He fills the earth continually. He does that for the earth and that is only one example of His work. Think about yourself, new blood, new skin and hair, etc. That is a picture of His great love for us. His mercies are new every morning, great, oh, great is His faithfulness!

DAY SEVEN

Joel 2:13 - "Return to the Lord your God, for He is merciful and compassionate, slow to get angry and filled with unfailing love. He is eager to relent and not punish."

THE PROPHET JOEL REMINDED THE PEOPLE OF GOD'S PATIENCE, MERCY AND compassion. Oh, how He loves you. The last line of verse thirteen says that God is eager to relent and not to punish. He takes no joy in punishing His children. I know we might have imagined God sitting on His throne waiting for us to mess up so He can beat us up. But that is not in His nature as our God! He longs for us to return to Him and take full advantage of His mercy and compassion.

Even when Jesus walked the earth, He was full of compassion. He healed the sick, raised the dead and fed the men, women and children many times. He taught the disciples, and served by example how to share the good news. How did Jesus do this? He led them. He chose to spend time with them. Even when the disciples didn't have it all together. He did not give up on them. He prayed for them. Our God is full of mercy and compassion. We can ask for these qualities to become a part of our daily lives and continue to be more and more like Him.

DAY EIGHT

Ephesians 5:18 - "Don't be drunk with wine- because that will ruin your life. Instead, be filled with the Holy Spirit."

WINE IS TEMPORARY - IT TAKES AWAY CLEAR AND COHERENT THOUGHTS IF consumed in excess. Don't drink and drive for it could be to your detriment. All these warnings are against being drunk with wine. But oh how wonderful it is to be filled and filled to the overflow with the spirit. Being filled with the spirit gives you the ability to hear Abba's voice clearly. Being filled with the spirit brings the peace of God, His love and the other fruit of the spirit to the forefront and more accessible to us. Being filled with the spirit takes us deeper and we are able to carry out our assignment as we follow the lead of the Lord. When we are filled with the spirit all those distractions are no longer an issue, we are better equipped to do what we have been called to do.

Let me encourage you to increase your worship time. As you worship, spend time by allowing the Lord to minister to you. How much you draw from the well will determine how your heart will be filled to overflow.

DAY NINE

Romans 5:5 - "And this hope will not lead to disappointment for we know how dearly God loves us because He has given us the Holy Spirit to fill our hearts with His love."

"Oh how He loves you and me, Oh how He loves you and me. He gave His life, what more could He give. Oh how He loves you, oh how He loves me, oh how He love you and me." (Kurt Kaiser)

Our hope lies in the one who loves us dearly. The Holy Spirit fills our hearts but how does that happen? It begins with a thought! When we think about the death, burial and resurrection of Jesus, it brings us straight to the Holy Spirit. Jesus told the disciples that He had to go away and that the Comforter which is Holy Spirit would come to dwell with us. The role of Holy Spirit is that He is our helper, He dwells in us regenerating and renewing us. He fills us with joy. He leads us into righteousness. Most importantly, our wisdom comes through the Holy Spirit for us to understand spiritual matters. As we are led by Holy Spirit, we will never be disappointed.

DAY TEN

Romans 15:13 - "I pray that God, the source of hope, will fill you completely with joy and peace because you trust in Him. Then you will overflow with confident hope through the power of the Holy Spirit."

OUR SOURCE IS THE ALMIGHTY GOD WHO CREATED HEAVEN AND EARTH. Have you ever felt hopeless and at a loss for words? You could not articulate what you were feeling but it just was a feeling of unrest. It is in those times that we ought to turn to the master creator. When we lack peace and joy - when we are dissatisfied with our present state, Abba's arms are open wide ready to take us in.

You see, it is about trusting the one who knows why He made you. When you go to Him even when there are no words, just tears, groaning and pain - He gets it and understand all your heart speaks. Yes, our Father has first-hand experience. Jesus experienced pain in the garden before going to the cross. He wanted to know if the cup He had to drink from could pass Him by, but He said not His will but the will of the Father was to be done. Jesus suffered for us so we'll be saved. We can bring it all to Him and be rest assured that in Him we will find refuge and be confident that He cares for us and will bring us through victoriously.

PART III
RENEW

DAY ONE

II Corinthians 5:17 - "Therefore if any man be in Christ, he is a new creation; old things are passed away behold all thing are become new."

OLD THINGS ARE PASSED AWAY, AND WE TEND TO GET RID OF OLD THINGS. We get rid of clothing that we are no longer wear or furniture that has become worn out. We toss them or we give them to someone who likes to refurbish things. But in any case, we move all those things out and make room for the new things. We clear out the space, sometimes repaint the walls, give the room a new look. When we reduce our weight, we clear out our closets to make room for our new clothes. We rearrange the closet to get it ready. The same should hold true when we come to Christ; we are a new creation. The old ways are set aside, and we no longer have the appetite for what our lives used to be. The old nature is dead and the new nature takes its place. Our desires change and we begin to take on the characteristics of our Father. It does not happen overnight, rather it is a gradual process. Just like weight reduction takes time, our new life in Christ is a daily process of letting go of the old and taking on the new. Don't beat yourself up because you didn't do everything right. Be thankful for the small wins on a day to day basis. What are you thankful today? What is your win of the day? Spend some time thanking God for your win in Him.

DAY TWO

Psalm 51:10 - "Create in me a clean heart and renew a right spirit within me."

WHEN WE MESS UP AND DON'T DO ALL THAT WE WANT TO DO, WE CAN TAKE comfort in knowing that we can ask the Lord to cleanse us and to renew a right spirit in us. The word renew means to make new; restored to freshness, vigor or perfection. When we come to the Lord and ask for His cleansing, our heart is restored, we receive a new freshness, wow! Imagine a new heart! We are renewed by the power of the Father. David asked for a clean heart. The meaning of created is to bring into existence-something that did not exist before. That is what we can ask for. We can thank God for a new heart, one that did not previously exist and to restore a fresh vigor in our spirit. We are like a computer that is refurbished. We send the damaged computer to the manufacturer and they take out the no good parts, sweep it clean and make it better than it was before. That is exactly what God will do for us. We have to go through the process of the old things being removed.

It may not feel good, but the end result is that we are better than we were before. Thank you Lord for making us new. What the Lord is saying to you is to let things go so you can be renewed.

DAY THREE

Psalm 51:12 - "Restore unto me the joy of thy salvation and uphold me with thy free spirit."

WE CAN AT TIMES IMPRISON OURSELVES WHEN WE DON'T FOLLOW ALL THAT the Lord has told us to do. We sin and then we feel bad, but we don't feel like we want to talk to about it. We are disappointed in ourselves - angry because we did it and get frustrated about this thing we call the Christian life. We now think that we are now in Christ, and we are supposed to be perfect. So what do we do? Let's take our cue from David. He sinned. He blew it big time. He got a woman that was not his wife pregnant, then killed her husband to cover it up and THEN he was confronted by the prophet. Nathan comes to him about his sin. Then David had to go to the place he should have gone in the beginning. He went to Abba, Daddy God, and laments his sin. He asks for restoration. He asked to be renewed in his spirit. He asks for forgiveness. No longer does he want to carry this burden of sin. He had been walking around without joy and peace, and this is similar to us when we have disobeyed God. What a privilege it is to know that we can come to God even when we mess up and we have the ability to come before Him and ask for restoration. And get this, He gives us just that immediately He restores us. He brings us back to Himself. We read that as far as the east is from the west that is how far He tosses our sins away! Just ask, don't suffer in silence. Come to God and come quickly. He waits patiently for you to restore you. Don't put off for tomorrow what you can do today!

DAY FOUR

Romans 12:2 - "And be not conformed to this world but be ye transformed by the renewing of you mind, that you may prove what is that god, acceptable and perfect will of God."

WHEN WE WANT TO DO SOMETHING IN LIFE THAT WE HAVE NEVER DONE before, it first starts as a thought. We sit in a meeting and our mind begin to wonder on how to do something better. It starts as of thought and we begin to think about it more and more; we start imagining how this thing can work. It gets bigger and bigger. But then we share it with someone and they rip our idea to shreds. At that point, we are at a crossroads. Do we listen to the outside voice or do we hold fast to our vision? When we know that the Lord has placed something in us, we must be willing to go against the grain and be renewed in our mind to do what will be an unpopular thing but the will of God.

DAY FIVE

II Timothy 1:6 - "Wherefore I put thee in remembrance that thou stir up the gift of God, which is in thee by putting on of my hands."

WHAT DO YOU HAVE IN YOUR HANDS? WHAT THING DO YOU LOVE TO DO? What are you excited about? When someone brings up a certain topic do your eyes light up? Just as surely as you get excited, do you second-guess yourself? Well, I have good news for you! Today is the day! I remind you to take hold of that gift within you and dust it off, take it off the shelf and begin to use it. Stir it up! Yes, take your gifts and let it be useful to those who need it. People have been waiting just for you to show up! They are waiting to be poured into by what you are carrying. No matter how big or small you may think your gift is, know this; what you have is necessary. What you have is needed. You cannot afford to waste God's gift. Yes, it is God's gift given to you and it is no good staying wrapped up. It must be unwrapped and set out in plain sight for the world to see and for those called to you to be changed!

DAY SIX

Isaiah 40:30,31 - "Even youths grow tired and weary, and young men stumble and fall; but those who hope in the Lord will renew their strength. They will soar on wings like eagles; they will run and not grow weary, they will walk and not be faint."

"You're too young to be so tired," I would hear those grown folks say to young people. They tell them that they haven't lived long enough to be tired! It made me wonder if people are tired because of what they are doing or how they are doing it. According to our scripture, if we wait on the Lord, He will renew our strength, we will gain additional strength to finish the task. Then you can go fast-run-not get weary and walk even when it gets a little hot outside and not faint. Do we move when we want to or do we move in sync with the direction of the Lord? We can sometimes get ahead of ourselves, so it is key to move with the rhythm of Holy Spirit. Let's move to His beat, and I believe that we will always have this strength to do what must be done. We won't waste time, energy or effort and Abba will get all the praise! Thank you Father for leading me!

DAY SEVEN

Ephesians 4:23, 24 - "..throw off your old sinful nature and your former way of life, which is corrupted by lust and deception. Instead, let the Spirit renew your thoughts and attitudes. Put on your new nature, created to be like God—truly righteous and holy."

WHAT ARE YOU SAYING? ARE WE SPEAKING WORDS OF LIFE OR ARE WE speaking words that condemn? The Scriptures tell us that we will be judged by the words we speak. Remember the old saying if you do not have anything nice to say, then don't say anything at all? It is still true today. We want to speak words of life - words that affirm and not condemn. You see, sometimes we are speaking out of turn. We may be saying something that may have been true of the person before but that is not who they have become. They have changed, grown, matured and are not the same person when you met them for the first time.

They are a new person - We have to see them through a new lens.

So the conversation has to change our interactions with them and it needs to match who they have become.

Maybe you are the person who changed or you are not the same individual anymore. You are transformed and you, yes you, must change the way you speak about yourself. Know who you are, affirm it daily by changing your personal conversation. Reflect on who God has made you to be today. What are some words you will now use to describe who you have become?

DAY EIGHT

II Corinthians 4:16 - "Therefore we do no lose heart that, but though our outer man is denying yet our inner man is being renewed day by day."

OUR BODIES CHANGE - WE ARE NOT THE SAME WHEN WE WERE 10 OR WHEN we were newborns. So we should not lose heart. We should be thinking of how good it is that our minds are daily thinking more and more about the things of God and how we can be more like Him. We should be thinking of how we can be examples to others and lead them to Christ. As we continue to memorize scripture, as we pray and listen for divine instruction, we are renewed in the body, soul and spirit.

Yes, we eat right and exercise to take care of our physical bodies. We realize that each year we continue to mature; things change - maybe our body shape or our hair color may change. Although that may happen on the outside, oh what a joy to know that our relationship with God has deepened within. We grow closer and we build more intimate relationship day by day. Thank you Father, you are so good!

DAY NINE

Colossians 3:10 - "And have put on the new self which is being renewed in knowledge after the image of its creator."

'Look at me I have been set free all my sins are washed away my night is turned today all because Christ has set me free.' - Tremaine Hawkins

New day, new dawning! Every day we are blessed with new mercies. We get the opportunity to do what God passes for us to do. We put on the new self, but what does that look like? It means we make the daily declarations of the day. We affirm who we are in Christ. We get our daily bread for the assignment that is at hand. When we get up in the morning, we read our Bibles and focus on a passage that we can meditate on that day. We allow the word of God to give us fresh revelation of who we are. It is wonderful to allow the word to envelop our spirit.

It is a blessing to know that we get to spend time with our supreme giver and praise Him for all He has done in and through us. God is great and greatly to be praised! For what will you thank Him today?

DAY TEN

Titus 3:5 - "He saved us, not because of works done by us in righteousness, but according to His own mercy, by the washing of regeneration and renewal of the Holy Spirit."

Isn't it good to know that our good works did not save us? The Bible says that our righteousness is as filthy rags before God. It was the mercy of God that washed our sins away! The indwelling of Holy Spirit brought salvation to our souls. We have been changed because we have Christ in us who is our hope of glory. He made us new. We are new in Him, made free and accepted in the family of the Most High!

We have been regenerated. I often think about when the power goes out in a neighborhood. There are some neighbors that have generators available in their houses, so even though the power goes out all around them, they can still function. They turn on the generator and they are back in business. We walked around in darkness without a Savior. But Jesus died and rose again, thereby giving us access to be regenerated. That word regeneration means "utilization by special devices of heat or other products that would **ordinarily be lost**." Had it not been for Jesus, we would "ordinarily be lost." Thank God for regeneration! "I once was lost but now I am found, I was blind but now I see!!!!!!"

ACKNOWLEDGMENTS

For the many people in my life who have influenced me, pushed me, motivated me and inspired me to bring this book to fruition, I say a huge thank you.

To all my coaches that have poured into my life I want to thank you all for speaking into my life and encouraging me not to give up. I will never forget all of the lessons you have taught me.

Dr. Saundra Wall Williams, you have taught me about focus, locating the main thing in ministry, discipline and structure. You have helped me put systems in place that allow me to be more deliberate and intentional in fulfilling God's call on my life.

Apostle Shirley R. Brown, my spiritual mother and mentor, I thank you for showing me how to prioritize, set things in order and do the right thing at the right time. You gave of your time to encourage, instruct, correct and push me into my Destiny. You have poured into me in so many ways and I will be forever grateful.

I started to name people who have walked with me while I was in the writing process and the list got longer and longer! I knew at that point that I was going to leave someone out so I want to say a huge "Thank You" to all of my friends and family that helped to keep me on task, especially my accountability partners, I so appreciate your push!

To my Grace Worship Center Church family, you all are fantastic and I am blessed to be on this ministry journey with you. To my family members, I know I have the absolute greatest family in the world! Our hearts are knitted together. I love each and every one of you.

To my loving husband Kevin, a godly man who constantly tells me that I can do it, I love you with all my heart. Your words of wisdom helped me focus on the important things. With you there walking with me, the journey is one filled with triumphs!

My world changer young adults - Kevin, II and Kennedy Elayne, you two are radiant lights and I am thankful that God gave you both to us.

ABOUT THE AUTHOR

Pastor Darlene Thorne has been devoted to ministry since she was in her early twenties with a desire to impart the word of God to those seeking a life change. This however, has not come without a price. She was raised in a Christian home with her two older sisters and younger brother. Her father was a pastor and her mother was an evangelist. They came together after graduating from Bible college.

After many years of marriage her parents divorced and Darlene was left with a question, "If her parents were believers and their marriage did not last, was God really real and what hope of living a solid Christian life did she really have?" Although she still knew God existed, Pastor Darlene struggled to know of His reality in her life. For some time after her parent's separation, Darlene led a very promiscuous life, she was at odds with her mother and felt abandoned by her father.

Not until she attended a conference which focused on teaching both children and adults how to have a successful and God-filled life, did Pastor Darlene make a total commitment to God and turned her life toward Him.

She experienced a new life in Christ that stripped away the bondage and she was delivered from rejection, low-self-esteem and she began to live life with purpose. Her assignment is to encourage women through God's word to live their lives with purpose and not to allow their past to be a hindrance.

As an international speaker, Pastor Darlene has traveled extensively ministering the word of God, speaking at conferences, seminars, workshops and women's meetings. She has a heart for women to be healed and truly be purposeful in their daily lives. To that end, she has authored two books, "A Heart After the Father," a daily devotional and "When Dark Chocolate is Bittersweet". She is presently working on a program entitled, "Slaying the Goliath's in Your Life," a series that examines major areas in our lives that war against us in our quest to fulfill our calling and a battle plan to win against one of our worst enemies, ourselves.

Pastor Darlene has been married to the love of her life for over 30 years. She and her husband, Kevin Thorne, serve together as pastors at Grace Worship Center in Clayton, NC. They have two world changer young adults, Kevin, II and Kennedy Elayne.

CONFERENCE TOPICS

Some of Pastor Darlene's conference topics are:

* You Weren't Designed to Fit In
   * The Me Nobody Knows
   * Hiding No More
    * Living Authentically: Embracing the Real You
   * How to Personally Invest in Your Dreams

www.ingramcontent.com/pod-product-compliance
Lightning Source LLC
Chambersburg PA
CBHW071438020526
44118CB00049B/2126